Revealing the Truth about
Angels and Demons

How God's angels help us fight and win our battles against Satan and his demons

Bright Kusinyala

Kingdom Books
Your kingdom come, your will be done

© 2013 by Bright Kusinyala

Published by Kingdom Books, an imprint of CreativeJuicesBooks, Singapore (www.creativejuicesbooks.com)

All rights reserved. No part of this book may be reproduced, stored in a retrieval system, or transmitted in any form or by any means — electronic, mechanical, digital, photocopy, recording, or any other — except for brief quotations in printed reviews, without prior permission in writing from the publisher.

All Scripture quotations, unless otherwise indicated, are taken from the *Holy Bible: New International Version* ®. Copyright © 1973, 1978, 1984 International Bible Society. Used by permission of Zondervan Bible Publishers. All rights reserved.

Scripture quotations marked (NLT) are taken from the *Holy Bible, New Living Translation*, copyright © 1996. Used by permission of Tyndale House Publishers. All rights reserved.

Scripture quotations marked (ASV) are taken from the *Holy Bible, American Standard Version*.

Scripture quotations marked (KJV) are taken from the *Holy Bible, King James Version*.

All emphases added to Scripture quotations are the author's.

National Library Board, Singapore Cataloguing-in-Publication Data

Kusinyala, Bright, 1980-
   Revealing the truth about angels and demons : how God's angels help us fight and win our battles against Satan and his demons / Bright Kusinyala. – Singapore : Kingdom Books, [2013]
      pages cm
      ISBN : 978-981-07-7211-6 (paperback)

   1. Angels – Christianity. 2. Demonology – Biblical teaching. 3. Spiritual warfare. I. Title.

BT963
235 -- dc23   OCN853603427

Cover design by Dave Elmert. Front cover depicts Archangel Michael vanquishing the devil; from a painting by Bonifacio Veronese.

Contents

	Foreword	1
	Introduction	3
1.	The Two Realms	5
2.	Spirit Beings	7
3.	Angels	9
4.	How to Tell an Angel from a Demon	17
5.	Satan	22
6.	Demons	26
7.	People	32
8.	The Two Kingdoms	38
9.	Jesus	46
10.	The Spirit Realm Rules over the Natural Realm	60
11.	Anointing of the Holy Spirit	78
12.	Refilling of the Holy Spirit	84
13.	*Seek the Lord Jesus*	89
14.	*Sinner's Prayer*	91

I dedicate this book to my Lord and Saviour Jesus Christ of Nazareth.

Secondly, I dedicate it to my wife Eurita, with whom I have won many spiritual battles. I also dedicate it to my son Nathan and daughters Felicia and Natalie.

I give special recognition to my mother Esther, who taught me the way of the Lord from a very young age. I also recognize the men and women of God who have made an impact on my spiritual life and helped me reach where I am today: Pastor Peter Tan, George Baros, Dr TL Osborn, Edir Macedo, Kenneth E Hagin, Ernest W Angley, and many others.

God bless you all.

Foreword

Pastor Bright Kusinyala is the founder and overseer of Regeneration Ministries International. He is married to Eurita Kusinyala and they have three children — Felicia, Nathan and Natalie.

Pastor Kusinyala received his call from God in 1992, at the tender age of twelve. His father was at that time working as a diplomat for the Malawian government in Addis Ababa, Ethiopia. One day, as Bright Kusinyala was preparing to go to school, he heard the Holy Spirit speak to him in a strong, convicting way. This was what the Spirit said: "I am calling you into a miracle ministry like my servant Reinhard Bonnke, and I shall manifest myself in healings and deliverances and miracles as you carry my Gospel of salvation to the nations. You will serve me when you are ready."

When his whole family returned to Malawi in 1994, Bright Kusinyala gave his life to Christ at a Gospel crusade in Blantyre where foreign evangelists had come to conduct crusades. Soon after that, he committed himself to serving God in various Pentecostal churches. He also ministered as an evangelist, holding miracle services for the Assemblies of God and other denominations.

In his first years of ministry, Pastor Kusinyala served as an Evangelist due to his initial calling. Later, in 2002, God added the office of a Teacher to his ministry and he worked with various teaching ministries. Then, in 2005, God added the office of a Prophet to his ministry.

Regeneration Ministries International was born in 2009 after Pastor Kusinyala had been serving in part-time ministry for ten years. Today, Regeneration Ministries is one of the fastest growing ministries in Africa, with almost 4,000 people attending its services. This is due to the signs and wonders that God is doing in its midst.

Pastor Kusinyala is very experienced in the healing, deliverance and prophetic ministries. Those of us who know him have seen the manifestation of demons in the services during his deliverance ministrations when he ministers to the oppressed. We have also seen the operation of angels in his ministry.

This is a practical book that shows how Pastor Kusinyala has availed himself of the help given by God's angels to heal many and deliver them from the devil's oppression. It also shows readers how they too can do likewise.

Elvis Ching'oma

Introduction

We are surrounded by millions of invisible beings that influence our daily lives and activities. These invisible beings are angels and demons. In this book, readers will gain valuable insights into what these angels and demons are doing in the lives of people today.

We read daily in the newspapers and magazines of children being abducted, teenagers found in possession of illegal substances, people committing horrendous crimes, countries at war, and many other distressing events taking place around the world. We ask ourselves, "Why are all these things happening?"

The answer is simply that we are surrounded by spirit beings that highly influence the activities and events in our lives. You are a spirit being that has a soul and lives in a human body. That makes it impossible for you not to be influenced by the spirit world: either by God and His angels or by Satan and his demons.

This influence is so real and so powerful that it manifests itself in the physical world in the thoughts you think and the decisions you make, the activities you carry out, and the events in your life — whether good or bad, depending on who is influencing you.

God impressed upon me to write this book in order to equip every believer with the knowledge of the activities taking place in the spirit realm. In the following pages, the spirit world is exposed so that you will gain insights into what God and His angels are doing on your behalf; and you will also find the evil deeds and plans of Satan and his demons laid bare so that you can be forewarned and take steps to safeguard yourself against them.

Dear reader, it is my prayer that, through this book, you will learn how to avail yourself of the help and protection that the angels of God are ever ready to give you; and you will also learn how to live victoriously by using your God-given authority and power over the enemy.

Pastor Bright Kusinyala

The Two Realms

There are two realms in life: the spiritual realm; and the natural or physical realm. The spiritual realm is of course invisible to the natural realm. God has created these two realms, and they complement each other:

> [G]iving thanks to the Father, who has qualified you to share in the inheritance of the saints in the kingdom of light. For he has rescued us from the dominion of darkness and brought us into the kingdom of the Son he loves, in whom we have redemption, the forgiveness of sins.
>
> He is the image of the invisible God, the firstborn over all creation. **For by him all things were created: things in heaven and on earth, visible and invisible, whether thrones or powers or rulers or authorities;** all things were created by him and for him. He is before all things, and in him all things hold together.
>
> *Colossians 1: 12-17*

We can see from the above Bible passage that Jesus created both the visible (physical) and invisible (spiritual) realms and He had a plan for both of them.

Many people think that life is all about the physical or natural realm, and they ignore the spiritual realm. **In reality, the spiritual realm is actually more real and more powerful than the physical realm.** The whole physical realm is highly influenced by the spiritual realm.

Everything that we see was actually first birthed in the spiritual realm. Let us take for instance the chair that you may be sitting on. It started as an idea in the mind of the manufacturer. That idea may have been put there by the Holy Spirit in the form of wisdom. I am saying "in the form of wisdom" because wisdom comes from God:

> If any of you lacks wisdom, he should ask God, who gives generously to all without finding fault, and it will be given to him.
>
> *James 1:5*

Spirit Beings

Both the spiritual and natural realms are governed by laws and inhabited by beings — spirit beings in the spiritual realm and physical beings in the natural realm. And God is the Father of all spirit beings:

> Moreover, we have all had human fathers who disciplined us and we respected them for it. How much more should we submit to the **Father of our spirits** and live!
> *Hebrews 12:9*

The Word of God also says explicitly that God is a spirit:

> **God is Spirit**, and his worshippers must worship in spirit and in truth.
> *John 4:24*

However, although God is a spirit, He is also the Creator of the physical universe. He is able to reveal himself in physical form too, when He so wills — as He did to Abraham (*Genesis 18:1-33*) and Jacob (*Genesis 32:24-30*).

But angels are only servants. **They are spirits** sent from God to care for those who will receive salvation.

Hebrews 1:14 (NLT)

Angels and demons are spirit beings too. God created angels but some of them rebelled against Him. Lucifer, one of the archangels, led the rebellion. Today, Lucifer is known as Satan and all the fallen angels are called demons.

God did not create the devil but He created angels and gave them free will; they were free to choose whether to submit to Him or rebel against Him.

Similarly, God has also given us free will, and we can choose to accept or reject Him.

Angels

Angels are spirit beings; they are at times in the Bible also called "sons of God" (*Genesis 6:2, 4; Job 1:6, KJV*). This is correct because the Bible says in *Hebrews 12:9* that God is the Father of our spirits. Angels are spirits, so they are also referred to as sons of God.

> Moreover, we have all had human fathers who disciplined us and we respected them for it. How much more should we submit to the **Father of our spirits** and live!
>
> *Hebrews 12:9*

God created a great host of angels of different ranks, and He gave them different assignments. He created worship angels like the Seraphim, messenger angels like Gabriel, and warrior angels like Michael; also ministering angels and guardian angels. In terms of types, the Bible records Seraphim with six wings, Cherubim with one pair of wings and other angels with no wings at all.

The Bible reveals that God has a very large population of angels; I believe they are so many as to be uncountable. That is why God can send angels to guard every human being on earth.

> I watched as thrones were put in place and the Ancient One sat down to judge. His clothing was as white as snow, his hair like whitest wool. He sat on a fiery throne with wheels of blazing fire, and a river of fire flowed from his presence. **Millions of angels** ministered to him, and a **hundred million** stood to attend him. Then the court began its session, and the books were opened.
>
> Daniel 7: 9-10 (NLT)

> "Put your sword back in its place," Jesus said to [his disciple], "for all who draw the sword will die by the sword. Do you think I cannot call on my Father, and he will at once put at my disposal **more than twelve legions* of angels?**"
>
> Matthew 26: 52-53

> Then I looked again, and I heard the singing of **thousands and millions of angels** around the throne and the living beings and the elders.
>
> Revelation 5:11 (NLT)

---

* *A legion in the Roman army comprised 6,000 soldiers.*

In my own life, I have encountered angels while I was fasting and praying. But it took many years for that to happen — at least ten years of being a believer. When we yield ourselves to the Holy Spirit and He starts to manifest His gifts in us according to *1 Corinthians 12: 8-10*, we can begin to see angels through the gift of discerning of spirits or the word of knowledge. These are the gifts of revelation that can give us insights into the spiritual realm.

The ministry of angels

The Bible says of angels:

> Are not all angels **ministering spirits sent to serve those who will inherit salvation**?
>
> *Hebrews 1:14*

Angels are sent by God to minister to us. They are mostly invisible but they can reveal themselves if God permits them. When the Lord was teaching me about His Word, there were times when He sent angels to give me information about the ministry that I am involved in today. Sometimes these angels appeared in the form of ordinary men and at other times as men in white robes and bright apparel.

I knew they were God's angels because the messages they spoke were in line with the Bible. If they had said something contrary to scripture, I would have known they were demons; and I would have commanded them in the name of Jesus to go!

Every revelation has to be examined in the light of God's Word (the Bible). The Spirit of God and the Word of God must agree. Paul says in *Galatians 1:8* that, if any angel comes to preach a different gospel from the one we have received through the biblical apostles, he must be cursed.

Some preachers, who are full of unbelief or who fear demons too much, preach that angels only appeared to people before Christ. This is erroneous because we see angelic ministration throughout the whole Bible, from Genesis to Revelation. In fact, a great deal of it occurred in the early Church, as recorded in the Book of Acts — as the following passages clearly show:

> The high priest and his friends, who were Sadducees, reacted with violent jealousy. They arrested the apostles and put them in the jail. But **an angel of the Lord came** at night, opened the gates of the jail, and brought them out. Then he told them, "Go to the Temple and give the people this message of life!"
>
> *Acts 5: 17-20 (NLT)*

> Now **an angel of the Lord said to Philip**, "Go south to the road — the desert road — that goes down from Jerusalem to Gaza."
>
> *Acts 8:26*

> At Caesarea there was a man named Cornelius, a centurion in what was known as the Italian Regiment. He and all his family were devout and God-fearing; he gave generously to those in need and prayed to God regularly. One day at about three in the afternoon he had a vision. **He distinctly saw an angel of God**, who came to him and said, "Cornelius!"
>
> *Acts 10: 1-3*

There are countless passages in the New Testament that talk about angelic ministration. Even though the Holy Spirit is present, God still uses angels to undertake specific tasks. They work in response to prayer.

> Another angel, who had a golden censer, came and stood at the altar. He was given much incense to offer, **with the prayers of all God's people**, on the golden altar in front of the throne. The smoke of the incense, together with **the prayers of God's people, went up before God from the angel's hand**.

Then the angel took the censer, filled it with fire from the altar, and hurled it on the earth; and there came peals of thunder, rumblings, flashes of lightning and an earthquake.

Revelation 8: 3-5

Angels come in response to our prayers

Angels are sent by God in response to our prayers. There is a close connection between prayer and angelic ministration. The Bible says that when Peter was in prison, the church prayed earnestly for him and this produced a miraculous result. God responded to their prayers by sending an angel to rescue Peter.

Peter was kept in prison, but **the church was earnestly praying to God for him**.

The night before Herod was to bring him to trial, Peter was sleeping between two soldiers, bound with two chains, and sentries stood guard at the entrance.

Suddenly an angel of the Lord appeared and a light shone in the cell. He struck Peter on the side and woke him up. "Quick, get up!" he said, and the chains fell off Peter's wrists.

Then the angel said to him, "Put on your clothes and sandals." And Peter did so. "Wrap your cloak around you and follow me," the angel told him. Peter followed him out of the prison, but he had no idea that what the angel was doing was really happening; he thought he was seeing a vision.

They passed the first and second guards and came to the iron gate leading to the city. It opened for them by itself, and they went through it. When they had walked the length of one street, suddenly the angel left him.

Acts 12: 5-10

In the Book of Daniel, too, we see God sending an angel when Daniel fasted and prayed.

At that time I, Daniel, mourned for three weeks. I ate no choice food; no meat or wine touched my lips; and I used no lotions at all until the three weeks were over.

On the twenty-fourth day of the first month, as I was standing on the bank of the great river, the Tigris, I looked up and there before me was a man dressed in linen, with a belt of the finest gold around his waist.

> His body was like chrysolite, his face like lightning, his eyes like flaming torches, his arms and legs like the gleam of burnished bronze, and his voice like the sound of a multitude.
>
> *Daniel 10: 2-6*

Notice it was after fasting and prayer that Daniel moved into the spirit realm and saw the angel. Earlier in the Book of Daniel, there weren't many revelations; but as he moved deeper into the prophetic office, he started seeing angels.

Angels have ministered to God's people in their times of need, and even to our Lord Jesus Himself. When Jesus was praying in agony on the Mount of Olives before His crucifixion, an angel came and strengthened Him:

> [Jesus] knelt down and prayed, "Father, if you are willing, take this cup from me; yet not my will, but yours be done." **An angel from heaven appeared to him and strengthened him**.
>
> *Luke 22: 41-43*

How to Tell an Angel from a Demon

The Bible teaches us:

> Don't forget to show hospitality to strangers, for some who have done this have entertained angels without realizing it!
>
> *Hebrews 13:2 (NLT)*

You never know when God might send an angel visibly into your life. I mentioned earlier that angels are always coming in and out of your life when you pray, but they are usually invisible. Here we are talking about the rare occasions when they come visibly into the life of a believer.

When you receive an angelic visitation, it is important to discern whether the angel is from God or not. You do this, first, by the inward witness of the Holy Spirit in you; second, by activating the gift of discerning spirits mentioned in *1 Corinthians 12:10*; and third, by the message spoken by the angel.

The inward witness of the Holy Spirit refers to the inner conviction that God places in your heart, or spirit. *Proverbs 20:27* says that the human spirit is the Lord's searchlight or lamp. God confirms things in our spirit: for example, whether an angelic visitation is from God or not.

We can also activate our gift of discernment. The ability to discern between the spirits is mentioned in *1 Corinthians 12:10* as one of the gifts of the Holy Spirit.

> To one person the Spirit gives the ability to give wise advice; to another he gives the gift of special knowledge… and to another the ability to prophesy. He gives someone else the **ability to discern whether a message is from the Spirit of God or from another spirit**… It is the one and only Holy Spirit who distributes these gifts. He alone decides which gift each person should have.
>
> *1 Corinthians 12: 8, 10-11 (NLT)*

The gift of discernment grants us insights into the realm of spirits and enables us to perceive if an angel is from God or Satan; and when the Holy Spirit wants us to, we can even see visions or hear the spirits. Discernment of spirits is a gift that powerfully equips us to engage in spiritual warfare.

We need also to check if the message spoken by the angel is in line with the Word of God.

Many people have been deceived because they listened to evil spirits disguised as angels. *Galatians 1:8-9* says every angel who preaches a gospel different from the Gospel of Christ is doomed to eternal punishment.

Satan is an intelligent being and he knows how to deceive us. Only in the Word of God do we find safety; any revelation or visitation contrary to the Word of God is demonic. Every angelic visitation has to line up with the Word of God, by the witness of at least two scriptures. This is to avoid revelations that are taken out of context.

The devil is a master at taking God's Word out of context so as to lead people into error. He succeeded with Adam and Eve in Eden, and he again tried it on Jesus in the desert. But Jesus knew the Scriptures well and wasn't deceived.

> Then Jesus was led by the Spirit into the desert to be tempted by the devil. After fasting forty days and forty nights, he was hungry. The tempter came to him and said, "If you are the Son of God, tell these stones to become bread."
>
> Jesus answered, "It is written: 'Man does not live on bread alone, but on every word that comes from the mouth of God.'"
>
> *Matthew 4: 1-4*

It is also important to remember that angels are not to be worshipped at any time. God is the only One we should worship:

> Again, the devil took him to a very high mountain and showed him all the kingdoms of the world and their splendour. "All this I will give you," he said, "if you will bow down and worship me."
> Jesus said to him, "Away from me, Satan! For it is written: '**Worship the Lord your God, and serve him only.**'"
> *Matthew 4: 8-10*

> Do not let anyone who delights in false humility and the worship of angels disqualify you for the prize. Such a person goes into great detail about what he has seen, and his unspiritual mind puffs him up with idle notions. He has lost connection with the Head…
> *Colossians 2: 18-19*

We are not supposed to seek after angelic visitations because Satan is a fallen angel who can disguise himself as an angel of light:

> Even Satan can disguise himself as an angel of light.
> *2 Corinthians 11:14 (NLT)*

The devil knows how to transform himself into an angel because he is an ex-angel and he knows how to shine like an angel too. That is why many people have been deceived into believing that an "angel" appeared to them. Sometimes, they were given demonic messages by these "angels", and that is how many religions began.

The Bible shows us how to distinguish between an angel and a demon:

> But even if we or an angel from heaven should preach a gospel other than the one we preached to you, let him be eternally condemned!
> *Galatians 1:8*

Demons appear the same as God's angels, but their messages are not in line with the Word of God. That is why we should not seek after angelic visitations. We should simply yield ourselves to the Holy Spirit and, if He wills, He can enable us to see God's angels through the gifts of revelation mentioned in *1 Corinthians 12*: namely, the word of knowledge, the word of wisdom and discerning of spirits.

Satan

Satan is the prince of demons. He is an ex-angel and the demons are also ex-angels who sided with him in his rebellion against God. The Lord Jesus called Satan "the prince of this world":

> "Now is the time for judgment on this world; now the prince of this world will be driven out."
>
> *John 12:31*

> I will not speak with you much longer, for the prince of this world is coming. He has no hold on me...
>
> *John 14:30*

The devil is also called Lucifer. *Isaiah 14* tells us how Lucifer fell from heaven: he wanted to exalt himself to the status of God, but his pride led to his downfall.

> How art thou fallen from heaven, O Lucifer, son of the morning! How art thou cut down to the ground, which didst weaken the nations!
>
> For thou hast said in thine heart, I will ascend into heaven, I will exalt my throne above the stars of God: I will sit also upon the

mount of the congregation, in the sides of the north: I will ascend above the heights of the clouds; I will be like the Most High.

Yet thou shalt be brought down to hell, to the sides of the pit.

Isaiah 14: 12-15 (KJV)

In *Ezekiel 28*, we learn more about the fall of Satan:

"Son of man, weep for the king of Tyre. Give him this message from the Sovereign LORD:

"You were the perfection of wisdom and beauty. You were in Eden, the garden of God. Your clothing was adorned with every precious stone — red carnelian, chrysolite, white moonstone, beryl, onyx, jasper, sapphire, turquoise, and emerald — all beautifully crafted for you and set in the finest gold. They were given to you on the day you were created.

"I ordained and anointed you as the mighty angelic guardian. You had access to the holy mountain of God and walked among the stones of fire. You were blameless in all you did from the day you were created until the day evil was found in you. Your great wealth filled you with violence, and you sinned. So I banished you from the mountain of God. I expelled you, O mighty guardian, from your place among the stones of fire.

"Your heart was filled with pride because of all your beauty. You corrupted your wisdom for the sake of your splendour. So I threw you to the earth and exposed you to the curious gaze of kings. You defiled your sanctuaries with your many sins and your dishonest trade. So I brought fire from within you, and it consumed you. I let it burn you to ashes on the ground in the sight of all who were watching."

Ezekiel 28:12-18 (NLT)

This long passage explains how Lucifer fell from grace and how he was transformed from a cherub (a type of angel) to the devil he is today. In the last paragraph, we read that God caused a fire to come out of him and consume him, turning him from the most beautiful angelic being into an ugly, demonic monster.

In the Book of Revelation, we have another account of the demons' fall from heaven.

> Then another sign appeared in heaven: an enormous red dragon with seven heads and ten horns and seven crowns on its heads. Its tail swept a third of the stars out of the sky and flung them to the earth.
>
> *Revelation 12: 3-4*

The devil is represented as a dragon, and the "third of the stars out of the sky" he flung to the earth refers to the one-third of the angels who joined him in his rebellion against God. Stars represent angels here, just as in *Isaiah 14:13*, where Lucifer is reported as saying he will place his throne above the stars of God.

The Book of Revelation tells us that Lucifer and his demons fought with the angels who had remained loyal to God, and that Satan's side lost and was cast out of heaven:

> Then war broke out in heaven. Michael and his angels fought against the dragon, and the dragon and his angels fought back. But he was not strong enough, and they lost their place in heaven. The great dragon was hurled down — that ancient serpent called the devil, or Satan, who leads the whole world astray. He was hurled to the earth, and his angels with him.
>
> *Revelation 12: 7-9*

Demons

Demons are fallen angels and, as I have mentioned earlier, angels operate in different ranks. When the demons fell, they kept their rankings and operated in those ranks under Satan. Demons of a higher rank got stuck in the heavens, whereas others fell to the earth and began to operate there.

The Bible gives us further insight into the operations of demons. In the Book of Ephesians, Paul lists them in four different ranks, from the lowest all the way up to the highest:

> For our wrestling is not against flesh and blood, but against the **principalities**, against the **powers**, against the **world-rulers of this darkness**, against the **spiritual hosts of wickedness in the heavenly places**.
>
> *Ephesians 6:12 (ASV)*

The four demon ranks

1. **Principalities** are the lowest order and demons of this rank carry out instructions given to them by the higher ranks. They work in big groups to cause as much destruction as they can.

2. **Powers** are the second-lowest rank of demons and they rule over the lowest, the first group. They operate in smaller units and are more powerful than the principalities.

3. **Rulers of darkness** are the largest and most powerful of the demons that fell to the earth (the fourth rank got stuck in the heavenly places). The Bible specifically says that they rule this world, which is why they are called "world-rulers". It is this type of demon that knows how to enter the spirit of a person and possess him or her completely, unlike the other demons that are less powerful.

4. **Spiritual wickedness in the heavenly places** refers to the highest rank of demons, but they do not operate on the earth. When they were cast down, they got stuck midway in the second heaven — and there they have remained, trying to block angels who bring help to people on earth.

Demon dominators

The first three ranks of demons — principalities, powers and rulers of darkness — are also called dominators because they seek to enter human beings and dominate them. Demons do not have bodies; so, when they want to operate on the earth, they seek a human body to enter and dominate. The highest dominators are the rulers of darkness; a good example is seen in Mark Chapter 5:

And when [Jesus] was come out of the boat, straightway there met him out of the tombs a man with **an unclean spirit**, who had his dwelling in the tombs: and no man could any more bind him, no, not with a chain; because that he had been often bound with fetters and chains, and the chains had been rent asunder by him, and the fetters broken in pieces: and no man had strength to tame him.

And always, night and day, in the tombs and in the mountains, he was crying out, and cutting himself with stones.

And when he saw Jesus from afar, he ran and worshipped him; and crying out with a loud voice, he saith, What have I to do with thee, Jesus, thou Son of the Most High God? I adjure thee by God, torment me not.

For he said unto him, Come forth, **thou unclean spirit**, out of the man.

Mark 5: 2-8 (ASV)

I have deliberately italicised the words "an unclean spirit" in the passage above. "An" means "one" in English; so the man was possessed by only one demon. But if you read the rest of the story, you will notice that this same man had thousands of demons which left him and entered into a herd of pigs:

> And he asked him, What is thy name? And he saith unto him, **My name is Legion; for we are many**. And he besought him much that he would not send them away out of the country.
> Now there was there on the mountain side a great herd of swine feeding. And **they** besought him, saying, Send **us** into the swine, that **we** may enter into them.
> And he gave **them** leave. And the **unclean spirits** came out, and entered into the swine: and the herd rushed down the steep into the sea, in number about **two thousand**; and they were drowned in the sea.
> *Mark 5: 9-13 (ASV)*

The man was possessed by a high-ranking demon, a ruler of darkness called Legion, who represented thousands of lower-ranking demons — all of whom were also in the man.

The same story is told in *Luke 8: 27-33*; and here again we see Legion, the ruler of darkness, dominating the man and ruling over many evil spirits in him. But rulers of darkness are still not the most powerful of demons.

Spiritual wickedness in the heavenly places

The highest-ranking and most powerful demons inhabit, not the earth or man, but the "heavenly places" — the second heaven. When Satan and his fallen angels were cast down, the most powerful of those demons were caught in the second heaven, and there they have remained.

There are actually three heavens. The **first** is the one we can see with our physical eyes, and it includes the one scientists travel to, when they go to the moon in spaceships and rockets; it is in the physical realm. The **second** heaven is the one where some of the demons got stuck in, when they fell from God's heaven. The **third** and highest is God's heaven, the exact place to which Paul was caught up in one of his revelations:

> Let me tell about the visions and revelations I received from the Lord. I was **caught up into the third heaven** fourteen years ago.

> Whether my body was there or just my spirit, I don't know; only God knows. But I do know that **I was caught up into paradise** and heard things so astounding that they cannot be told.
> *2 Corinthians 12: 1-4 (NLT)*

The demons in the second heaven are always trying to block God's angels who are on their way from the third heaven to earth, bringing answers to people's prayers. This was what happened to the prophet Daniel; the angel sent to him was delayed by a demon for twenty-one days. Here is what the angel said:

> "Don't be afraid, Daniel. Since the first day you began to pray… your request has been heard in heaven. I have come in answer to your prayer. But for twenty-one days the spirit prince of the kingdom of Persia* blocked my way. Then Michael, one of the archangels, came to help me, and I left him there with the spirit prince of the kingdom of Persia*."
>
> *Daniel 10: 12-13 (NLT)*

---

* The "spirit prince of the kingdom of Persia" refers to the demon who exercised influence over the Persian realm.

People

Everyone is a spirit living in a body

Every one of us is a spirit that has a soul and lives in a body. This is why, though we live in the physical world, we are highly influenced by the spiritual realm. We are fully spirit and fully physical, unlike any animal on the earth. The Bible says clearly that man is a spirit (or that he has a spirit), as is evident from the references below (I have placed the word *spirit* in italics wherever it refers to the spirit of man):

> The *spirit* of a man will sustain his infirmity; But a broken *spirit* who can bear?
>
> *Proverbs 18:14 (ASV)*

> The *spirit* of man is the lamp of Jehovah, searching all his innermost parts.
>
> *Proverbs 20:27 (ASV)*

> The grace of our Lord Jesus Christ be with your *spirit*, brothers. Amen.
>
> *Galatians 6:18*

> For if I pray in tongues, my *spirit* is praying, but I don't understand what I am saying.
>
> *1 Corinthians 14:14 (NLT)*

The Bible distinguishes between the spirit of man (small "s") and the Holy Spirit (capital "S"):

> The Spirit himself testifies with our *spirit* that we are God's children.
> *Romans 8:16*

We can tell that we are spirit beings because we are able to dream when our bodies are asleep. Though your mind may be unconscious during sleep, your spirit remains wide awake and it is your spirit that dreams. Your spirit never sleeps because a spirit never gets tired, like a physical body does.

Your dreams reveal much about your life: it can pick up satanic attacks against you, the hidden desires of your heart, and also divine signals from God. Dreaming is very important to all of us because it alerts us to things in the spirit that we may not be able to perceive with our physical senses. When you are oppressed by the devil, you can easily know it by the kind of dreams you dream at night; this enables you to seek prayer and deliverance.

We are merely visitors on earth, spirits living in bodies that are temporary, like a tent. Everyone on earth needs a physical body to live in. Your body enables you to live on earth; it is like a suit you put on. This suit is a biological machine, functioning according to the biological laws of the earth.

Upon death, the spirit leaves its earthly body and enters the spirit world, either descending to hell or ascending to heaven. For us — if Jesus is our Lord and Saviour — we can say, like the Apostle Paul, that to die is to be home in heaven with Christ.

> But our citizenship is in heaven. And we eagerly await a Saviour from there, the Lord Jesus Christ, who, by the power that enables him to bring everything under his control, will transform our lowly bodies so that they will be like his glorious body.
>
> *Philippians 3: 20-21*

We all need Jesus

Upon the death of its physical body, a spirit will either descend to hell or ascend to heaven. Only those who have accepted Jesus as their Lord and Saviour will go to heaven. It is therefore of utmost importance that you make Jesus your Lord and Saviour; if you have not done so, I urge you to **turn at once to page 91 of this book and pray the prayer you see there.**

When you make Jesus your Lord and Saviour, three things happen. The Word of God says that, first, you have heard (or read) the proclamation of God's salvation; second, you have believed in your heart that God raised Jesus from the dead and He is able to save you; and, third, you have confessed that Jesus is the Son of God.

> But what does it say? "The word is near you; it is in your mouth and in your heart," that is, the word of faith we are proclaiming: That if you confess with your mouth, "Jesus is Lord," and believe in your heart that God raised him from the dead, you will be saved. For it is with your heart that you believe and are justified, and it is with your mouth that you confess and are saved.
> *Romans 10: 8-10*

You believe with your heart (that is, your spirit) and confess with your mouth (that is, your physical body). Thus, accepting Jesus as Lord and Saviour is an act that involves both your spirit and your physical body. This applies also to all other prayers that you and I pray; you believe in your heart or spirit, and you speak with authority using your physical mouth — and you will be victorious in Jesus' name!

We are created in God's image

The Bible tells us we are created in God's image:

> Then God said, "Let us make people in our image, to be like ourselves. They will be masters over all life — the fish in the sea, the birds in the sky, and all the livestock, wild animals, and small animals."
>
> So God created people in his own image; God patterned them after himself; male and female he created them.
>
> *Genesis 1: 26-27 (NLT)*

The Bible further tells us that Jesus is the visible image of the invisible God.

> May you be filled with joy, always thanking the Father, who has enabled you to share the inheritance that belongs to God's holy people, who live in the light. For he has rescued us from the one who rules in the kingdom of darkness, and he has brought us into the Kingdom of his dear Son...
>
> Christ is the visible image of the invisible God. He existed before God made anything at all and is supreme over all creation.
>
> *Colossians 1: 11-13, 15 (NLT)*

Philip said, "Lord, show us the Father and that will be enough for us."

Jesus answered: "Don't you know me, Philip, even after I have been among you such a long time? Anyone who has seen me has seen the Father."

John 14: 8-9

So, if human beings were created in God's image and Jesus is the image of the invisible God, it follows that they were created in the image of Jesus. Yes, it was God's idea from the beginning, and it is still His plan for all who come to Him, that they be conformed to the image of His Son:

For those God foreknew he also predestined **to be conformed to the image of his Son**, that he might be the firstborn among many brothers and sisters.

Romans 8:29

Dear friends, now we are children of God, and what we will be has not yet been made known. But we know that **when he [Christ] appears, we shall be like him**, for we shall see him as he is.

1 John 3:2

The Two Kingdoms

Two kingdoms exist in the spirit realm: **the kingdom of darkness**, headed by Satan; and **the kingdom of light**, headed by God. Everyone who has not accepted Jesus as Lord and Saviour is in the kingdom of darkness, and is influenced by it and by its demons. Those who follow Jesus as their Lord and Saviour have passed from the kingdom of darkness into the kingdom of God.

> [G]iving joyful thanks to the Father, who has qualified you to share in the inheritance of his holy people in the kingdom of light. For he has rescued us from the dominion of darkness and brought us into the kingdom of the Son he loves, in whom we have redemption, the forgiveness of sins.
> *Colossians 1: 12-14*

Two kingdoms control the natural realm

The spirit realm greatly influences the natural realm. For those in the kingdom of God, prayer is the connection between God and man. Angels move in to complement this connection by bringing God's answers to our prayers. As for those in the kingdom of Satan (even if they are atheists): they are in darkness, their minds controlled by demons; this is evidenced by sin and ungodliness in their lives.

No one is independent of the spirit realm. Satan and his cohorts are in a desperate battle to ensnare souls in order to take them to hell. God, on the other hand, is drawing people to Himself through the wonderful Gospel of Jesus Christ; He is delivering many out of the kingdom of darkness and giving them a relationship with Himself.

The two kingdoms are engaged in a fiercely fought war, and their battleground is the physical realm. Satan and his demons influence the world to do evil, whilst God and His angels influence people to pursue holiness and godly living. The devil manifests his presence through sickness, disease and death; but, when Jesus steps in, He gives life, healing and hope to the nations.

> The thief comes only to steal and kill and destroy; I [Jesus] have come that they may have life, and have it to the full.
>
> *John 10:10*

The kind of life Jesus gives is different from man's ordinary life; the Greek translation for it is

Zoe. It means God energizing every part of a person's life, with physical, emotional and spiritual health and blessings — just as He promised in His Word.

How to avoid demonic influences

When people do evil, it is often because they are under the influence of demons. To avoid demonic influences, we must meditate on the Word of God and the things of God. We must guard our thoughts, for the thought life is the doorway through which the spirit realm enters and influences us.

> Since, then, you have been raised with Christ, set your hearts on things above, where Christ is seated at the right hand of God. Set your minds on things above, not on earthly things. For you died, and your life is now hidden with Christ in God.
> *Colossians 3: 1-3*

> Finally, brothers and sisters, whatever is true, whatever is noble, whatever is right, whatever is pure, whatever is lovely, whatever is admirable — if anything is excellent or praiseworthy — think about such things.
> *Philippians 4:8*

The best way to avoid Satan is to do the will of God by obeying His Word, and also to rid your mind of all negative thoughts. The devil likes to take over our minds; he relays thoughts to human beings in the form of temptations. However, when your mind is renewed by the Word of God, you will be able to resist temptation, just as Jesus did:

> Then Jesus was led by the Spirit into the desert to be tempted by the devil. After fasting forty days and forty nights, he was hungry. The tempter came to him and said, "If you are the Son of God, tell these stones to become bread."
>
> Jesus answered, "It is written: '**Man does not live on bread alone, but on every word that comes from the mouth of God.**'"
>
> Then the devil took him to the holy city and had him stand on the highest point of the temple. "If you are the Son of God," he said, "throw yourself down. For it is written:
>
>> "'He will command his angels
>>   concerning you,
>>   and they will lift you up in their hands,
>>   so that you will not strike your foot
>>   against a stone.'"

Jesus answered him, "It is also written: '**Do not put the Lord your God to the test.**'"

Again, the devil took him to a very high mountain and showed him all the kingdoms of the world and their splendour.

"All this I will give you," he said, "If you will bow down and worship me."

Jesus said to him, "Away from me, Satan! For it is written: '**Worship the Lord your God, and serve him only.**'"

Then the devil left him, and angels came and attended him.

Matthew 4: 1-11

Jesus' answers to the devil (highlighted above in bold) were drawn from the Book of Deuteronomy; I have again highlighted the relevant quotes below in bold:

Do not test the Lord your God...

Deuteronomy 6:16

Fear the Lord your God, serve him only and take your oaths in his name.

Deuteronomy 6:13

He humbled you, causing you to hunger and then feeding you with manna, which neither you nor your fathers had known, to teach you that **man does not live on bread alone but on every word that comes from the mouth of the LORD.**
Deuteronomy 8:3

The Lord always had an answer from Scripture to refute the lies of the enemy, and the devil fled. The Word of God tells us to resist the devil and he will flee from us (*James 4:7*).

Prayer is powerful against demonic activity

Earlier on we talked a little about prayer. Prayer is very powerful; it can change situations in both the spiritual and natural realms. When we pray, God sends angels to intervene on our behalf. They wage war against the forces of darkness, and secure victories for us in both the spiritual and natural realms. That's how we get answers to prayers and see changes in the physical realm.

We have not done everything we could possibly do, until we have prayed through our situations. Some problems in the natural realm cannot be solved no matter what you do physically; such difficulties can only be resolved through prayer. This is because invisible forces exist that control situations in people's lives.

As a pastor, I see God answering prayer every day. People come to me with different problems but God always intervenes when it is His will to do so.

The prayer of faith moves mountains

Jesus taught us in His Word that, even if we have only a little faith — as little as a mustard seed — we can move mountains. Faith in God produces fantastic results!

> [Jesus] replied, "Because you have so little faith. Truly I tell you, if you have faith as small as a mustard seed, you can say to this mountain, 'Move from here to there,' and it will move. Nothing will be impossible for you."
> *Matthew 17:20*

The Bible tells us that the prayer of faith can accomplish the impossible.

The prayer of faith heals the sick:

Is any among you sick? Let him call for the elders of the church; and let them pray over him, anointing him with oil in the name of the Lord:

And **the prayer of faith shall save him that is sick**, and the Lord shall raise him up; and if he have committed sins, it shall be forgiven him.
James 5: 14-15 (ASV)

The prayer of faith removes obstacles and changes situations in people's lives:

"Have faith in God," Jesus answered.

"Truly I tell you, if anyone says to this mountain, 'Go, throw yourself into the sea,' and does not doubt in their heart but believes that what they say will happen, it will be done for them. Therefore I tell you, **whatever you ask for in prayer, believe that you have received it, and it will be yours.**"

Mark 11: 22-24

Jesus

Jesus is God

The Bible states clearly that Jesus is God:

In the beginning was the Word, and the Word was with God, and **the Word was God**. He was with God in the beginning.
  Through him all things were made; without him nothing was made that has been made. In him was life, and that life was the light of all mankind.
John 1: 1-4

So the Word became human and lived here on earth among us. He was full of unfailing love and faithfulness. And we have seen his glory, the glory of **the only Son of the Father.**
John 1:14 (NLT)

For the law was given through Moses; God's unfailing love and faithfulness came through Jesus Christ. No one has ever seen God. But his only Son, **who is himself God,** is near to the Father's heart; he has told us about him.
John 1: 17-18 (NLT)

The same Jesus who said, "Before Abraham was, I AM" (*John 8:58*) is also the "I AM", the God who spoke to Moses in the burning bush:

> God said to Moses, "I AM WHO I AM. This is what you are to say to the Israelites: 'I AM has sent me to you.'"
>
> *Exodus 3:14*

Jesus is the Saviour of the world

God sent His Son Jesus into the world to save everyone who believes in Him:

> For God so loved the world that he gave his one and only Son, that whoever believes in him shall not perish but have eternal life. For God did not send his Son into the world to condemn the world, but to save the world through him.
>
> *John 3: 16-17*

Everyone in this world has sinned and gone far away from God. Jesus came to die for us and reconcile us to God.

> For the grace of God that brings salvation has appeared to all men. It teaches us to say "No" to ungodliness and worldly passions, and to live self-controlled, upright and godly lives in

this present age, while we wait for the blessed — the glorious appearing of our great God and Saviour, Jesus Christ, who gave himself for us to redeem us from all wickedness and to purify for himself a people that are his very own, eager to do what is good.

Titus 2: 11-14

Christ also suffered when he died for our sins once for all time. He never sinned, but he died for sinners that he might bring us safely home to God. He suffered physical death, but he was raised to life in the Spirit.

1 Peter 3:18 (NLT)

Jesus will save all who call on His name and take Him as their Lord and Saviour.

Everyone who calls on the name of the Lord will be saved.

Romans 10:13

If you have not asked Jesus to be your Lord and Saviour, I urge you to **turn to page 91 of this book and pray the prayer you see there**.

Jesus answers prayer today

Jesus has assured us that He will answer our prayers:

> "Keep on asking, and you will receive what you ask for. Keep on seeking, and you will find. Keep on knocking, and the door will be opened to you. For everyone who asks, receives. Everyone who seeks, finds. And to everyone who knocks, the door will be opened."
>
> *Matthew 7: 7-8 (NLT)*

As a pastor, I often see the Lord Jesus answering prayer in powerful and amazing ways. I have seen Him intervening in "impossible" situations and turning them around; I have seen Him healing sicknesses for which there was no known medical cure; I have seen Him setting people free from demonic possession. I myself have also been healed by Him on several occasions. I therefore stand as a witness that Jesus answers prayer today:

> "But you will receive power when the Holy Spirit comes on you; and you will be my witnesses in Jerusalem, and in all Judea and Samaria, and to the ends of the earth."
>
> *Acts 1:8*

Jesus heals the sick today

Jesus has healed me of several serious and incurable diseases, and I have seen Him heal others too. The first time was when I was in my teens. My brother Stewart and I had developed itchy eyes, and the doctors said it was a hereditary allergy. I was fifteen then, and my brother was only twelve. We were told that there was no remedy and we would have to use eye drops all our lives for relief.

Having accepted Jesus at a young age, I believed that He could heal me — and He did. I approached a pastor and told him that if he prayed for me I knew I would be healed. As soon as he laid hands on my head, I received my healing. My brother Stewart was healed too, when anointing oil was poured on him — just as it had been promised in the Bible:

> Is anyone among you sick? Let them call the elders of the church to pray over them and anoint them with oil in the name of the Lord. And the prayer offered in faith will make the sick person well; the Lord will raise them up. If they have sinned, they will be forgiven.
>
> *James 5: 14-15*

Many years later, before I went into full-time ministry as a pastor, I worked for Coca-Cola in their sales department. It was a very stressful job and I ended up with high blood pressure. The doctors said I would have to go on long-term medication but I refused. Instead, I fasted and prayed for three days and three nights. That was the end of the high blood pressure; I got healed and I am still healed today.

Apart from these two incidents, there were other occasions when Jesus healed me; all of these experiences remain as testimonies of God's healing power in my life because I am still enjoying divine health today.

As a pastor, I receive over 3000 people for prayer every week. They come with diverse kinds of sicknesses and diseases, and the Lord Jesus has proven His Word to be true by healing many of them.

I love to see Jesus heal the sick. There is no sickness that He cannot heal; He heals **all** diseases with no exception. The following passage from the Book of Isaiah makes it clear that healing was part of God's purposes for us when Jesus made atonement on our behalf.

> **Surely he took up our infirmities**
>   and carried our sorrows,
> yet we considered him stricken by God,
>   smitten by him, and afflicted.
>
> But he was pierced for our transgressions,
>   he was crushed for our iniquities;
> the punishment that brought us peace
>   was upon him,
> **and by his wounds we are healed**.
>
> We all, like sheep, have gone astray,
>   each of us has turned to his own way;
> and the LORD has laid on him
>   the iniquity of us all.
>
> Isaiah 53: 4-6

As a pastor, I have challenged the crowds during church services and told them to bring the blind and deaf up to the front — and God has healed these people of their infirmities before the very eyes of the whole congregation! Once, a young boy of about twelve years old, who had never spoken since birth, came up to the front with his uncle. I asked the crowd, "Do you believe Jesus can do this?" They shouted a resounding "Yes!"

I told the boy to stick out his tongue, then I touched it with my finger and said, "You dumb spirit, come out in the name of Jesus!"

Then I told him to repeat words after me. He repeated them without difficulty. He said the words, "Baby, mommy, one, two, three", and even counted up to ten. The crowd gave a shout of praise to Jesus, and some even broke down and cried tears of joy.

On another occasion, a famous Malawian Gospel musician by the name of Maggie Mangani came to our church service, carrying her younger sister. The girl was in her late teens, but had been sick and could not walk. She had to be carried in by three women, and she was moaning and breathing heavily, almost at the point of death. Everyone was watching me to see my reaction to such a situation.

Knowing that Jesus was with me and placing my faith in His name, I knelt down where they had laid her and commanded, "You spirit of death and you spirit of infirmity, in the name of Jesus come out!"

I reached out and put my hands on the girl's head and feet, and commanded strength to enter her. Then I stood up and said, "Young lady, in the name of Jesus rise up because you are healed!"

She got up and started walking in front of everybody, completely healed. People began shouting praises to Jesus.

Another young Malawian musician named Dwale Kalaya was also healed one afternoon after a service. He had been diagnosed as suffering from Kaposi's sarcoma (a type of skin cancer) and had a bandage wrapped around his neck. When he took off the bandage, I saw that his neck was covered with severe wounds caused by the cancer. I looked at him and sensed that the spirit of death was upon him.

I rebuked this spirit of death and commanded life to come into Dwale's body. I stretched out my hand towards him without touching him, and commanded the spirit of cancer to leave. He fell down under the power of the Holy Spirit and was delivered from the spirit of cancer.

A few days later the wounds dried up, and when he went to the hospital the doctor could not find any trace of cancer. It has now been more than a year since Dwale received his healing, and he remains cancer-free to this day.

Every single day I attend to the sick, and I see these miracles as a normal part of my life as a servant of God:

> He spoke, and they were healed — snatched from the door of death.
>
> *Psalm 107:20 (NLT)*

Jesus delivers babies too

One day a pregnant woman came to me with a pressing problem. Her baby was due but it was not in the normal head-down position; it was in what they call a breech presentation. She was told that a natural delivery was out of the question and she would have to go for a caesarean operation.

I spoke with authority and commanded the baby, in the name of Jesus, to assume a head-down position. And it did. Just 24 hours later, the mother went to the hospital for a check-up and, to everyone's surprise, the baby was found to be in a head-down position. Throughout my years of experience as a pastor, I have seen several cases similar to this one. I ministered in the same way to all of them and each time the Lord Jesus came and upended those babies.

Another time, I was about to start preaching at a Wednesday afternoon service when some members of our church committee came barging in. They cried, "Pastor, we have an emergency that needs your urgent attention!"

I rushed out of the service and saw a pregnant woman in terrible pain. Her baby was long overdue but could not come out. I had no idea what to do, so I laid my hand on her head and started to pray. I said, "In the name of Jesus, I decree that labour starts for delivery of the baby!"

Less than five minutes later, the woman went into labour — and it was a very short labour of only three minutes before she delivered her baby right in front of me! That was a hair-raising moment for me. I can only thank God that there were experienced midwives around to help the woman.

Jesus delivers people from demons

The biggest enemy of man is the devil and his cohorts. Some people even become demon-possessed when they fall into Satan's snares. But Jesus is able to deliver them out of the devil's clutches:

> The reason the Son of God appeared was to destroy the devil's work.
> *1 John 3:8b*

When you attend our services, you will see mass healings take place, and also mass deliverances as demons fall down in manifestations and are cast out of people.

One day a demon-possessed woman came to ask for help. As I began to pray for her, she fell to the floor and the demons in her body went into manifestations of screaming and screeching. I commanded the demons to leave in the name of Jesus and the woman was set free.

She came back a few days later and told us that she used to work as a prostitute in the pubs. She had previously been diagnosed as HIV positive — having contracted the disease when she was a prostitute — and had decided to attend our deliverance service in the hope that God would heal her.

After her dramatic deliverance from demons, this woman went back to the hospital for more HIV tests. All the tests turned out to be negative this time round. She had been healed of the dreaded HIV virus! I then led her to receive Christ and today she is a great woman of God.

This woman is one of many that we have seen Jesus deliver from demonic bondages. In our services, we see the sick being healed in great numbers and devils being cast out. Many people have been saved, and even Muslims are surrendering their lives to Jesus Christ.

It has always been the will of God to heal the sick and deliver the oppressed, especially those suffering from demon possession. This is in accordance with the proclamation of Jesus Christ in His Word:

"The Spirit of the Lord is on me,
because he has anointed me
to preach good news to the poor.

He has sent me to proclaim freedom
for the prisoners
and recovery of sight for the blind,
to release the oppressed,
to proclaim the year of the Lord's favour."

Luke 4: 18-19

In Africa, there is a lot of witchcraft as well as other satanic activities going on. Demons use people supernaturally to bring about calamities in the lives of others. But Christians are now preaching the Gospel and Jesus is saving many who have been in bondage to demons. Jesus has power over all powers, and He is bringing deliverance to the devil's captives.

Some years ago I held a Gospel crusade at a village near the city of Blantyre. There, I saw multitudes in bondage because of witchcraft. A woman came up during the crusade and I saw that she had her neck embedded in her chest. She was not born like this but became deformed because she had been bewitched by her enemies. If you could have seen her, you would have been shocked at how her head and shoulders were touching each other!

During prayer, I commanded the spell of witchcraft to be broken in the name of Jesus. At once, her neck grew right out of her shoulders and she was restored. This miracle happened in front of multitudes of people, and many accepted Jesus as their Lord and Saviour that day.

On another occasion, after one of our services in the city, a woman came forward for prayer as she had a tumour in her private parts. I said a simple prayer, "In the name of Jesus, I command the tumour to disappear!" Later that evening she called my wife and me to say, "Pastor, I can't explain it but I can't find that tumour; it's just disappeared into thin air!" Glory to Jesus!

Jesus heals the sick today! He delivers the demon-oppressed! He answers our prayers!

Praise the Lord!

The Spirit Realm Rules over the Natural Realm

Problems caused by demons

Many problems are caused by demons, just as it says in the Word of God:

> For our wrestling is not against flesh and blood, but against the principalities, against the powers, against the world-rulers of this darkness, against the spiritual hosts of wickedness in the heavenly places.
>
> *Ephesians 6:12 (ASV)*

Demons try to influence us to sin so that they can control our lives and cause destruction. A demon can speak into our minds and tell us bad things about others. If we don't realize it's a demon speaking to us, we may start asking ourselves questions like, "Why am I having these bad thoughts?" or worse still, "Oh, how horrible So-and-so is!" — Not realizing that we are under the influence of a demon!

The devil is experienced in taking over people's minds. He can take over a man's mind and lure him into crossing a busy road and getting killed by on-coming traffic. He can take over a situation where people are angry and make them do what they didn't intend to do. This sort of thing happens to many people. When you ask them why they went out of control, they always say, "I don't know what came over me."

I heard of an incident where a man of God was walking along a road when he came across two men fighting. The Lord opened his spiritual eyes and he saw a demon with horns standing between the two men, acting like a referee in a boxing ring. The demon was egging the men on to fight even though they couldn't see it!

So, you see, the physical realm is influenced by the spiritual realm. If you look back at some disastrous events in your life, especially those where emotions or situations seemed to have escalated out of control, you will realise there was a demonic influence behind them.

A good example in the Bible is when King David wanted to take a census of the soldiers of Israel. There was a spiritual influence that made King David come up with the idea of a census.

Satan rose up against Israel and incited David to take a census of Israel.

1 Chronicles 21:1

My dear reader, do you notice what is happening here? The Word of God makes it clear that it was Satan's idea for David to number Israel! This resulted in Israel being punished by God, and the angel of the Lord was sent to execute judgment against the whole nation (*1 Chronicles 21: 7-15*). It was Satan who instigated King David to conduct the census; his purpose was to make the king sin against God. This is one of many instances when events have ended in calamity because they were initiated by demons.

God and His angels protect us

The activities that originate from God and His angels have a very different end result from those initiated by demons. Many people have felt a great peace when demons have been cast out of them, and when the Holy Spirit takes over, He influences believers to live holy lives and make godly decisions. This in turn brings us God's blessings and His protection.

Have you ever been in a situation where something bad was about to happen but you managed to escape? That was because God protected you. The angels of God are here to protect us, and many times they enable us to escape the Devil's snares.

> The angel of the LORD encamps around those who fear him, and he delivers them.
>
> *Psalm 34:7*

The Devil lays traps for people, but when we walk with God He defends us:

> For he will rescue you from every trap and protect you from deadly disease.
>
> *Psalm 91:3 (NLT)*

Some Christians have escaped terrible accidents, storms, earthquakes and pestilences because God protected them. God has promised to deliver His children from all harm:

> [N]o evil will conquer you; no plague will come near your home.
>
> *Psalm 91:10 (NLT)*

God has protected me on more than one occasion. One day I happened to be in a car with my elder brother, who was a nonbeliever at the time. He was driving when he suddenly realised that the car's brakes were not working. He panicked as the car started to pick up speed going down a slope. I was very calm because I knew the Lord would deliver us. I began to pray and, all at once, a force stopped the car and we were saved.

Some years later I had another narrow escape that was just as dramatic. This happened when I was courting my wife Eurita. Her employer had posted her to a city about 400 kilometres away from where I was living at the time, and I would make trips by minibus to visit her. I didn't have a car then.

Returning home from one of my visits to Eurita, I was on a minibus barrelling along at 120 km per hour when the Holy Spirit prompted me to pray. I hadn't prayed more than a minute when the rear tyre on the left of the bus burst. Everybody started to panic as the tyre rim was now scraping the tarmac and the minibus — still travelling at 120 km per hour — was about to overturn.

Not wanting to take any chances, I shouted out, "In the name of Jesus, align yourself on three wheels and stabilise!" And the bus did just that.

I then said, "In the name of Jesus, stop!"

The minibus stopped and we were all safe. God had surely intervened in the situation. People started to praise the Lord as we got off the minibus to change the tyre. Nobody could deny that God had delivered us. God answers prayers, no matter how difficult our situation may seem.

God brings the dead to life

God answers prayers — no matter how impossible it may seem. God can even bring the dead back to life, as He has done for my family.

When my wife and I were expecting our daughter Felicia, we had to go on a trip to a nearby city to attend my cousin's funeral. On the way back from the funeral, my wife started complaining of severe abdominal pains. She was five months pregnant at the time. I rushed her to the hospital, only to be told by the doctor that she had a fibroid the size of a fist in her uterus.

The pain grew so severe she could not even stand up without help. The doctors injected painkillers into her to ease her pain, but the problem was that those painkillers affected the baby in the womb and its heart stopped beating. The only medical solution was to save the mother by operating on her to remove the baby and the fibroid.

My unborn daughter had been reported clinically dead, right in her mother's womb. For five days there was no heartbeat and my wife was in pain. The doctors told my wife's relatives that they needed to operate on her to remove both the baby and the fibroid. I wasn't at the hospital when this was discussed, but when I came I refused to allow anyone to operate on my wife. I insisted that God was going to intervene. I prayed for my wife and the fibroid disappeared. The baby also came back to life in her mother's womb — and today we have our beautiful daughter Felicia!

Someone may ask, "Can God do that? Bring the dead back to life?" My answer is a big YES!

Look at the following Bible passage, which refers to God's promise to Abraham. I want you to focus on the words in bold:

> As it is written: "I have made you [Abraham] a father of many nations." He is our father in the sight of God, in whom he believed — **the God who gives life to the dead** and calls things that are not as though they were."
>
> *Romans 4:17*

The God who gives life to the dead: these are not random words. Take a look at this other verse, which is also from the New Testament:

> For just as **the Father raises the dead and gives them life**, even so **the Son gives life** to whom he is pleased to give it.
>
> *John 5:21*

I want you to notice that both scriptures are in the present tense: "God who **gives** life to the dead"; "the Father **raises** the dead and **gives** them life"; "the Son **gives** life". It is therefore not something that only happened in the past or will only happen in the future, but *it is occurring now, at this present time.*

Moreover, it is the *simple* present tense form ("gives" and "raises') that is used, indicating that this raising of the dead is a habitual action that takes place all the time.

God is able to raise the dead, and He still does it today. My daughter is a living testimony of this. And, surely, if the Lord has worked such an awesome miracle for my family, He can do even greater things in your life!

Prophecies from the spirit realm

Whatever is in the physical realm is subject to change by the spirit realm. We can therefore conclude that the spirit realm is more powerful than the physical realm. The relationship between the spiritual realm and the physical realm may be likened to that between you and your image in the mirror.

Your mirror image cannot change unless the real you changes first: if you smile, your face in the mirror smiles back at you; if you raise your arms, your image will raise its arms too. Now, that's exactly how the two realms operate. Nothing can be changed in the physical or natural realm unless some activity takes place first in the spiritual realm.

Prophecy tells us that something has happened in the spiritual realm, and we can expect to see changes taking place in the natural realm as a result. For example, just before my Dad passed away, the Lord told my mother and me that He wanted to take my father home. My Dad had already suffered four strokes before this prophecy came. The day before he went to be with the Lord, God told me I wasn't going to see my father again. I was setting off for a nearby city and I had to spend the night there.

Having had this revelation, I said farewell to my Dad and kissed him goodbye before I left. There were tears in my eyes but I knew it had been settled with the Lord because my Dad had already received his salvation. His time had come and I had to let him go, although it was painful for me. Dad passed away exactly the next day, after I left the city.

Here is another prophecy I received. In 2003 I had a friend called Emmanuel. This friend of mine was courting a lady, and their courtship was about to lead into marriage; but before that could take place, the lady fell sick and my friend asked me to go to her home to pray for her. Somehow, I was not able to do so at the time as I had other commitments.

My friend Emmanuel decided to get his brother, who was a pastor, to pray for her. I too made intercession for her, when I was at home. However, the Holy Spirit spoke to me, saying, "Just pray for her salvation because this sickness is leading to her death."

That came as a shock to me, but I did as the Lord had said.

Two days later, Emmanuel called me and said, "Bright, my brother prayed for her and she is better already. Don't be bothered to come".

I was praying in my bedroom later that afternoon and the Lord spoke again. He said, "The young lady hasn't really recovered. It's only the symptoms of the disease that have disappeared but she will not recover from this sickness. Pray for her salvation."

A few days later, Emmanuel called me to say that she had fallen sick again and had been admitted to a hospital. While I was getting ready to visit her, the Holy Spirit told me not to go but to pray further for her repentance and salvation.

The next day, at around 12pm, I was praying in my living room when the Holy Spirit said, "Bright, the young lady has just passed away but she has made it into heaven. You will receive a call in exactly ten minutes from now to confirm this."

Exactly ten minutes later, I received a call from Emmanuel. He said, "Bright, she has passed away."

I replied that the Lord had already told me the whole story. In response, Emmanuel said that he had also met another servant of God who told him exactly what the Lord had told me: that she would not recover.

He had just been calling me to try his "luck", in case the situation could be changed.

Warnings from the spirit realm are sent to protect us

God and His angels watch over us and protect us; they may sometimes also warn us about impending dangers so that we can avoid them. This was what happened to me some years back.

In 2001 I was working for a radio station. One day, on my way home from work, I decided to take a shortcut through a particular road. As I was walking along the road, a man stepped right in front of me and told me to turn back — because, he said, about fifteen metres up ahead were five armed men lying in wait for unwary travellers.

At first I thought this was an ordinary man, but just after he had said those words, he disappeared. It was then that I realised he was an angel God had sent to warn me. I obeyed the angel's advice and turned back. I later discovered that there had indeed been five armed men waiting in ambush at that spot, on that day, ready to pounce on people passing by. I had been saved by an angel!

That wasn't a vision; the angel that appeared to me was very real — just like the angel who appeared to Peter in *Acts 12: 5-10.*

The Bible says in *Acts 12:9* that Peter thought it was a vision but the angel was there for real. In a vision, we use our spiritual senses to see into the spirit realm, but in this case an angel had manifested himself in the physical realm and Peter could see him with his physical eyes. If anyone else had been present, they too could have seen the angel.

Listen to the Lord!

Sometimes God or His angels will try to warn us against making decisions that may ruin our lives. That was what happened to me some years ago, when I was dating a girl I thought I wanted to marry. The first time I met her, the Lord Jesus told me she wasn't a true born-again believer; but I answered Him by saying I wanted to prove it for myself. That was my biggest mistake.

The Word of God says to all believers:

Howbeit when he, the Spirit of truth, is come, he shall guide you into all the truth: for he shall not speak from himself; but what things soever he shall hear, these shall he speak: and he shall declare unto you the things that are to come.

John 16:13 (ASV)

In this case, the Spirit of God had already shown me things to come but I did not listen — and so I ended up disappointed. In the midst of our courtship, she ran off with the manager of a hotel.

In my disappointment, I began to fast and pray, seeking God for divine inspiration and direction. While I was on my knees, praying in my bedroom, the Lord Jesus appeared to me in a powerful vision. He was shining brilliantly, and His voice was like the sound of many waters, just like it said in *Revelation 1: 15-16.*

The first thing He said to me was that He had tried to warn me against this woman but I had failed to listen, and so He had let me have it my way. He said, "The heart is deceitful above all things and beyond cure. Who can understand it?" (*Jeremiah 17:9*)

After quoting that scripture to me He said, "You have been deceived by your heart. You let your heart deceive you that you were in love. I warned you the first time you met her, but you didn't want to listen."

Each time the Lord spoke to me, I felt strength enter my body and I felt a great comfort in my heart. The Lord was right; He had warned me right from the start. I should have listened to Him.

Learning from that experience, I began to pray for God's choice of a wife for me — and He directed me to my godly wife, Eurita. This time round, I made sure that I received specific directions from the Lord about who my wife was to be, and He was faithful; He gave me the desire of my heart!

That was not my only visitation from Jesus. He also appeared to me on other occasions, in order to prepare me for the ministry He had entrusted into my hands. I pastor Regeneration Ministry and I am the general overseer of this ministry. Our first service in 2009 was attended by only five people but today almost 4,000 people attend our services.

When Jesus appeared to me He did not always look the same. At times I saw Him as a bright light and the form of a man was in that light. On other occasions, He appeared to me in human form. In one of His visitations, He enabled me to see the activities of demons in the spiritual realm.

Activities of demons

The Lord Jesus woke me up at 3am in 2011. My wife was fast asleep and I didn't disturb her on the bed. In a split second Jesus and I were standing in a dark place, and I began to see strange-looking beings moving all around us. Those beings were demons and they looked horrifying. When I saw them, my hair stood on end.

The Lord Jesus spoke to me and said, "Don't be afraid, because you are not alone. I am with you and these demons cannot touch you. They cannot see you because you are standing with me."

I saw some of the demons carrying small transparent sacks. In the sacks I saw names of people, and the demons were rushing around and past us with those sacks. The Lord then explained to me that He had taken me to that place so that I could understand how demons operate. He told me that what I saw in the sacks were names of people whom the demons had been sent to attack.

The demons were all different in appearance; some had scales like reptiles while others were dark and ghostlike. But they all looked hideous, like what you would expect to see in horror movies. That's the best I can describe them.

The Lord explained to me that the spirit realm was exactly what I could see. It is a dark place, full of demonic forces. *Ephesians 6:12* says that we wrestle not against flesh and blood but against principalities, powers of darkness and rulers of darkness who rule this world, and spiritual hosts of wickedness in the heavenly places.

Demons act upon our words

After the Lord had shown me those demons, in the twinkling of an eye, I found myself in my bedroom again and my wife was still asleep. But this time Jesus was with me in the room and He said, "Do you notice anything here?"

I replied, "Lord, I don't see demons anymore."

The Lord Jesus looked at me and said, "When we were in the spirit realm, you could see the demons but they couldn't see you. Hear this: even though you don't see them now in the physical realm, they can see you and hear you.

"Go and tell my people that they need to be careful what they say because demons hear and act negatively upon negative words. They do it in just the same way that I and my angels act upon my word when people confess it.

"Demons act upon negative and bad words, and **angels act upon the confessed Word of God**. The demons you saw were carrying sacks with names of people who confessed negative things and they were acting upon those words.

"**Make my people understand the importance of being careful with their words,** like my Word says in the Book of Proverbs." (*Proverbs 10:19, 17:27, 29:20*)

A few days later I went on to share this with the people of God and they were edified.

Anointing of the Holy Spirit

In the year 2005, I had a visitation from an angel who came to talk to me about the anointing of the Holy Spirit. When the angel approached me, he told me that before the rapture there would be an increase of the anointing of the Holy Spirit in the Body of Christ. He then held my hand and, in the twinkling of an eye, we were standing in a huge church auditorium filled with people.

The angel told me to stand near the altar, and he left me there and moved towards the people. Whenever he got near the people, I saw cripples walking, people falling down and manifesting demons, and others falling down and getting healed. There was no physical contact between the angel and the people.

After this mighty demonstration of the power of God, the angel walked towards me and I felt a rush of power pushing me back a few steps, but I didn't fall. Then he told me, "This anointing will operate in the ministries of those men and women of God who remain faithful to Jesus before the rapture." He went on to say that, if I would remain faithful, God would entrust me with this kind of anointing.

In the past two years I have noticed that, whenever I fast and pray, God has increased the anointing upon my ministry. At times, even when a person who has a demon stares at me, the demon goes into manifestations. I then command it to come out in the name of Jesus. I am slowly reaching for higher and higher levels of this anointing of the Holy Spirit. I want to move from strength to strength, faith to faith, and anointing to anointing.

My greatest desire after salvation is to see *John 14:12* come to pass in my life, because this is one out of many of God's promises to us:

> Very truly I tell you, whoever believes in me will do the works I have been doing, and they will do even greater things than these, because I am going to the Father.
> *John 14:12*

The reason why I want this in my life is not to shine before others, but to help those who are suffering. I have seen many healed of terminal sicknesses like cancer and Aids. On the other hand, I have also seen some people die of these same diseases. I can safely say that, out of every two thousand sick people in a church, only five hundred get healed. This happens all over the world and it has led me to one conclusion: that we are not yet on the level where God wants us to function as His Church.

Another reason why we have prayed for so many people and they have still died is that we lack the power of God in our lives, to the extent that God expects us to have it. It is not because God didn't want to heal those people.

Let's face it, God is not a liar. If He gave us the mandate to continue His work on the earth in the same manner that He did — and to do even greater works, as *John 14:12* promised — then we are the ones failing to do the work. Jesus has given us the same Holy Spirit that He had, but we are still not doing the same works He did, not to mention the greater works we are supposed to do.

I believe another reason why we are unable to do the works God has called us to do is that the Church en masse has "spiritualised" the simple, straightforward meaning of *John 14:12* and given it another meaning to justify our failure. Some say that the "greater works" mentioned in that scripture verse refer to preaching through the mass media, such as on satellite television and the internet. However, I strongly believe that Jesus was not talking about preaching using technology.

Our Lord said that we shall do the *same works* He had done, and even greater works. The works He had done, and which we should be doing, include healing the sick and maimed, casting out devils, and raising the dead. Those works created an impact, and Jesus used them to evangelise and draw people into the kingdom of God.

Recently the Lord has been talking to me in great detail concerning these works. When Jesus was on the earth, He healed ALL who came to Him for ministration:

> And all the multitude sought to touch him; for power came forth from him, and healed them **all**.
>
> *Luke 6:19 (ASV)*

I want you to notice that *all* were healed in the ministry of Jesus but, in church services around the world today, only *some* are healed. Furthermore, the healings done by Jesus were all of a high quality. The Word of God categorises the types of miracles that Jesus did: healing of the lame, blind, dumb and maimed. These healings were all creative miracles, involving the replacement of missing limbs and organs. The lame — those who were crippled — had their legs replaced so they could walk; the blind were given new eyes that could see; the dumb had new tongues to speak with; and the maimed who had lost limbs or body organs were given new ones.

> And there came unto him great multitudes, having with them the lame, blind, dumb, maimed, and many others, and they cast them down at his feet; and he healed them.
>
> *Matthew 15:30 (ASV)*

These miracles also happen today but on a smaller scale because people are satisfied with the little they receive. God wants to do more, and He is looking for willing vessels — people who will go all the way with Jesus.

When we look at the ministry of the apostles, we can see that they actually grew from healing a few people to healing all who came to them. That's what the Church needs to do today.

When they first started out, the apostles healed only *some* of the people, just like we are doing today:

> They went out and preached that people should repent. They drove out many demons and anointed many sick people with oil and healed them.
>
> *Mark 6: 12-13*

Notice that they cast out "many devils" and healed "many sick people" — *many but not all*. A little later in the Book of Mark, we see that the disciples failed to cast out a particular kind of demon, despite the authority Jesus had given them earlier:

> A man in the crowd answered, "Teacher, I brought you my son, who is possessed by a spirit that has robbed him of speech. Whenever it seizes him, it throws him to the ground. He foams at the mouth, gnashes his teeth and becomes rigid. I asked your disciples to drive out the spirit, but they could not."
>
> *Mark 9: 17-18*

This is exactly what is happening in the Church today. Some diseases are being healed and some are not. The apostles, however, did not remain for long at that level of being able to heal only some and not all. Later in the Bible, we see them moving on to a higher anointing of the Holy Spirit, wherein they were able to heal *everyone* who came to them:

> And there also came together the multitudes from the cities round about Jerusalem, bring sick folk, and them that were vexed with unclean spirits: and they were healed **every one**.
>
> *Acts 5:16 (ASV)*

Refilling of the Holy Spirit

When the Lord Jesus appeared to me, He taught me that it is one thing to be filled with the Holy Spirit and it is another to be *full of the power of the Holy Spirit*. Many believers have received the baptism of the Holy Spirit, with the initial evidence of speaking in other tongues. But since their baptism in the Holy Spirit, they have let their flame go out due to lack of prayer.

The Lord Jesus told me that the reason many people of God are not making any impact for His kingdom is that they are not living a life of sacrifice and sanctification unto God. After their baptism in the Holy Spirit, they are in haste to lay hands on others but sadly they see no results. The Lord pointed out to me Luke Chapter 4 as the key to moving in the Spirit. There are four observations to note here:

Let the Holy Spirit fill you

Jesus, **full of the Holy Spirit**, returned from the Jordan and was **led by the Spirit** in the desert…

Luke 4:1

First of all, Jesus was full of the Holy Spirit and He was led by the Spirit. Many believers do not remain full of the Holy Spirit after their baptism in the Holy Spirit. The Word of God commands us to be filled with the Holy Spirit:

> Don't be drunk with wine, because that will ruin your life. Instead, **let the Holy Spirit fill and control you.**
> *Ephesians 5:18 (NLT)*

When we talk of being filled with the Holy Spirit, it means being baptised by the Holy Spirit and remaining filled after the baptism. There is one baptism in the Holy Spirit but many refillings. A good example can be found in the Book of Acts. In *Acts 2:4*, the believers were all filled with the Holy Spirit and spoke in tongues; but in *Acts 4:31* the Bible says that the same believers had another filling of the Holy Spirit. That was a refilling.

Let the Holy Spirit lead you

Secondly — still on *Luke 4:1* — Jesus was led by the Spirit. Being filled by the Holy Spirit enables us to be led by the Spirit. The best way for a believer to remain filled by the Holy Spirit is to spend time on the Word of God and also to pray in the Spirit (praying in tongues). Praying in tongues is the doorway into the spiritual realm. The Bible tells us that it is not the babes in Christ but the older children who are led by the Spirit:

> For those who are led by the Spirit of God are the **children of God.**
> *Romans 8:14*

In the Bible, the words "son" and "daughter" refer to mature children who can be relied upon by their parents:

> "And afterward, **I will pour out my Spirit** on all people. Your **sons** and **daughters** will prophesy, your old men will dream dreams, your young men will see visions."
> *Joel 2:28*

There is always a leading from the Spirit of God when a person is full of the Holy Spirit.

Fast and pray for victory

Thirdly, Jesus fasted before starting His ministry:

> Jesus, full of the Holy Spirit, returned from the Jordan and was led by the Spirit in the desert, where for forty days he was tempted by the devil. He ate nothing during those days, and at the end of them he was hungry.
> *Luke 4: 1-2*

Some say He did it because He was the Messiah, but I don't believe that was His reason for fasting. Many Christians find a lot of excuses to run away from this kind of sacrifice (which is what fasting entails). They forget that, in everything Jesus did, He was setting an example for us to follow as believers.

Jesus is the Messiah but, when He was baptised by John the Baptist, He wasn't a sinner. He was showing us what we needed to do. In the same way, when He was baptised by the Holy Spirit near the river Jordan, He was showing us that we cannot be victorious unless we are filled with the Holy Spirit.

After His baptism in the Holy Spirit, our Lord did not start rushing around, laying hands on people. He needed the anointing of the Holy Spirit so that He could have power over sickness, disease and death. In *Mark 9:29*, Jesus told His disciples that some devils don't come out unless we fast and pray:

> [H]is disciples asked him privately, Why could not we cast him out?
> And he said unto them, **This kind can come forth by nothing, but by prayer and fasting.**
> *Mark 9: 28-29 (KJV)*

Fasting leads to anointing

Fourthly, the Holy Spirit anointed Jesus after His forty-day fast. The anointing of the Holy Spirit energises a believer to be used by God so that miracles can happen. This anointing comes to the believer as a result of fasting.

> Jesus returned to Galilee in the power of the Spirit, and news about him spread through the whole countryside.
> *Luke 4:14*

When Jesus fasted for forty days and nights, He was showing us how we can reach our full potential, so that we can utilise the gifts of the Holy Spirit to fulfil God's call upon our lives. I personally am a witness to the power of God that comes through fasting and prayer. When we fast and pray, we draw ourselves nearer to God, who rewards those who seek Him:

> [A]nyone who comes to him must believe that he exists and that **he rewards those who earnestly seek him**.
> *Hebrews 11:6*

The visitations I had from the Lord took place mostly during my days of fasting and prayer. I have had the most wonderful encounters with God in my life, and I believe such encounters should be a normal part of the life of every believer, where God so wills.

Seek the Lord Jesus

Jesus is the link between the physical realm and the spiritual realm. Through Him we know God because Jesus himself has said that no one can know God except through the Son.

Christianity is not a religion but a reality; and we can prove it is real because of God's faithfulness to His Word and His promises in the Bible. My exhortation to every reader is that you seek the Lord Jesus for yourself. With Jesus, you can change your world. It doesn't matter what your circumstances look like right now. The physical realm responds to the spiritual realm. All you need is to have God on your side:

> For every child of God **defeats this evil world by trusting Christ to give the victory**. And the ones who win this battle against the world are the ones who believe that Jesus is the Son of God.
>
> *1 John 5: 4-5 (NLT)*

Dear reader, when you have faith in Jesus, God will enable you to overcome the challenges of life; for with God all things are possible.

> For nothing is impossible with God.
>
> *Luke 1:37*

God will become a reality to you as you draw close to Him; and Jesus even promises to show Himself to you if you love and trust Him.

> Whoever has my commands and obeys them, he is the one who loves me. He who loves me will be loved by my Father, and I too will love him and show myself to him.
> *John 14:21*

This promise is not only for pastors or ministers of the Gospel, but also for every believer who is a child of God.

Everything has a starting point. Perhaps you may not know Jesus as your Saviour, or maybe you are a backslider. The best starting point is for you to ask Jesus to come into your life. You can do this by repeating the **Sinner's Prayer** on the next page. Say it and mean it with all of your heart.

If you have prayed that prayer with all of your heart, you are on the right track. You can now devote yourself to God in prayer and in reading His Word. You can now claim God's promises for your life and you can change your circumstances in the physical realm by trusting in the name of Jesus.

Sinner's Prayer

Dear Jesus, I am a sinner and I cannot help myself. Please forgive all of my sins and wash me in your precious blood. I renounce all of my sinful ways and I will follow you with all of my heart from now onwards. Satan has no power over my life anymore because, Jesus, you are now my Lord and Saviour.

Thank you, Jesus, for forgiving me my sins. I am now born again! I know that I now have a relationship with you, Jesus; and I have my right to health, prosperity, peace in marriage and all your promises.

Amen.

QUESTIONS? COMMENTS?

Write to:

Pastor Bright Kusinyala
Regeneration Ministries International

Email addresses:
kusinyalab@yahoo.com
brightkusinyala@yahoo.com
kusinyalab@gmail.com

www.ingramcontent.com/pod-product-compliance
Lightning Source LLC
Chambersburg PA
CBHW032020040426
42448CB00006B/679